The Comforting Theory of Time

A Rhythmic & Whimsical Reflection

By: Gary Kilmer

***A 40 minute read
that will change your Hour,
your Day, and your Life.***

As you read this, someone in your life may be navigating a difficult time, someone who could find comfort in these pages.

If you'd like to send this book as a gesture of kindness and support...

Please visit
www.TheComfortingTheoryOfTime.com
or scan the QR code below:

Foreword:

*When life is good, faith is easy.
What's not easy is holding on to one's ideals through a battle with heartbreak, depression, and uncertainty. In my case, during my young adulthood,
I experienced an emotional pain so complete that it shook my very faith
...in faith.*

*I lost my belief in Karma, in God, in "The Power of the Universe," "The Law of Attraction," and in all those "higher power" beliefs that hold us together in the difficult times when the fellow human beings in our lives
let us down. I lost faith in all of it.
For a while, I couldn't believe in anything.*

*But even when my trust in a higher power was shaken, my mind never lost the comfort it derived from my understanding of Time.
I realized that Time had never asked for my faith. It had always been there
moving forward,
whether I noticed it or not,
and that was enough.*

I didn't have to BELIEVE in anything. Time doesn't require belief. It doesn't require anything from me. It simply is what it is, undeniably, and to me that meant I didn't have to place my hope for better days in the hands of some intangible higher power, at least not at that moment. It gave me an undeniable constant, something I can always depend on, a place to safely rest...my faith.

So, with "The Comforting Theory of Time" swimming around as an unwritten and unspoken concept in the back of my mind, I pressed forward, step by step, day by day, scared to proceed, but terrified to stay where I was, knowing that time would eventually set me free.

Sometimes when something momentarily brings the pain of the past back to my present, I question whether I've been successful at "moving on?" Other times, the simple wonders of life bring me tears of joy and I'm reminded that I can FEEL again, and that feels good. (I really missed that.)

*It's then that
I'm reminded that I'm "there."
I'm past it. I'm now "looking back."*

*I haven't lost the hurt filled memories
(sometimes I wish I could), but I'm not
living daily in those
painful places anymore.
It happened. Time set me free.*

*Did Time itself and my understanding of
it become my personal "higher power?"*

*Perhaps. Temporarily.
(Until my faith in other sources
had time to heal.)*

*Either way, it worked,
and that's comforting.*

*This book is not about waiting for things
to change. It's about trusting time while
continuing to move forward,
even in small ways.
Progress doesn't have to be rushed.
It just has to exist.*

How to Read This Book...

(Yes. Really.)

"The Comforting Theory of Time" is meant to be read in a particular way.

- **Rhythmic** (ˈrɪð.mɪk) – *Having a deliberate, flowing cadence or pattern that guides the pace.*

- **Whimsical** (ˈwɪm.zɪ.kəl) – *Playful and imaginative in a way that invites curiosity and a sense of lightness.*

- **Reflection** (rɪˈflɛk.ʃən) – *A thoughtful and contemplative exploration of an idea, meant to inspire introspection and new perspectives.*

This book is intended as "A Rhythmic & Whimsical Reflection", inviting readers to engage with it in a slow, thoughtful manner. It encourages pauses and reflections between each page turn, allowing for breath, space, and a new (and more comforting) understanding of Time to resonate and transform your life.

The choice to print only a few words per page, (or in some cases, only one word per page), is intended to help you naturally fall into a calming and contemplative cadence. When approached in this way, the words can take on qualities of a Reflective Mantra.

- **Reflective Mantra** (rih-FLEK-tiv MAHN-truh) – *A carefully paced sequence of words meant to be read slowly and thoughtfully, allowing space for introspection, calm, and a shift in perspective over time.*

*If you find yourself with a physical copy of this book, try to set aside 40-50 minutes when you won't be disturbed. Find a comfortable spot or a quiet peaceful place where you can read it in one sitting. As you read, take your time, and consider the words (or word) on the page fully before gently turning to the next. You're going to find yourself in a relaxing rhythm that will allow your spirit to calm, and your mind...to be comforted.

**Should you find yourself reading this on a Kindle, E-reader, or other mobile device, don't miss out on the calming experience of reading this book as a rhythmic and reflective mantra. Consider adding a breathing regimen to everything I suggest above.
After reading each page, and contemplating the words (or word) therein, take a slow and intentional breath before scrolling to the next page.

*****

Let's Begin…

(Breathe)

Time.

*Time is
a constant.*

*You can't slow time,
speed up time or stop time.*

Neither can anyone else.

*That's how time
will always set you free.*

And that's...comforting.

*We're conditioned early to
think time is our enemy.*

We try:

>*to stretch it.*
>*to save it.*
>*to make it.*
>*to borrow it.*
>*to steal it.*
>*to cheat it.*
>
>*and even to kill it.*

But what if?

What if...we changed our understanding of Time?

What if?

We let time free us?

We let time save us?

What if?

*We viewed Time as the constant in our lives that **always** led to our happiness?*

(You can't slow time, speed up time or stop time.)

(Neither can anyone else.)

*If we let Time be the constant in our lives that **always** led to our happiness…*

That would be comforting.

*Time is not in
our control.*

*At first, that doesn't **seem**
very comforting.*

(Things we can't control often make us feel powerless and unsafe – right?)

But could that be comforting?

Since Time is unchanging in speed, and therefore unchanging in duration,

And if it is not in our control to alter that,

Then time is a constant in our ever changing lives.

Even during times of stress, pain, and uncertainty,

    I can depend on Time to always be the same.

(That's a little comforting.)

*So how can I depend
on time to always set me free?*

All things end.

We've all heard

*"All good things come
to an end."*

(Pessimistic)

So do the bad things.

(Realistic)

All things end.

(Eventually.)

*We don't know when
the bad things will end.*

*We don't know how
the bad things will end.*

But maybe that's not important?

(for right now)

Time is a constant.

We can depend on it.

*So as time ticks on,
we know those difficult times
will end.*

*We may not know how.
We may not know when.*

*But we don't need to question "if"
the bad things will end.*

They will end.

*No one has the power
to slow time.*

*No one has
the power to stop time.*

*So the question is never "if"
a bad situation will end.*

It will end.

Every bad situation will end with the dependable and constant passing of time.

And that's comforting.

It doesn't matter how it ends.

It doesn't matter when it ends.

*The comfort comes when you embrace the certain inevitability that it **will** end.*

No one can stop that.

That's how time will always set you free.

And just that little bit of knowledge...is comforting.

*The Comforting Theory of Time
is not about passively waiting for
your situation to change.*

It's about trusting Time itself,

patiently continuing forward,

and knowing that Time will deliver you...

to a moment when you'll look back and realize you've already moved beyond this.

It's a certainty.

*It **will** happen.*

Want an example?

(Let's keep it light.)

The talkative neighbor lady has "trapped" you again across the bushes with the tales of her latest doctor's visit.

(That's pretty light - right?)

She's a kind older lady, whose favorite past-time seems to be talking about her own health.

(Yep...You know "her.")

(We all know "her.")

*Just as she begins with
the intimate details of her
cholesterol count,*

*your eyes glaze over the curlers
in her hair, and a voice in your
head says*

"I'm going to be here forever."

That voice in your head is <u>not</u> very comforting.

*You remember the last
time this happened…*

*You suffered a full thirty minutes
listening to what medications
were taken when and why.*

*You wanted to die,
but instead, you smiled.*

It's now that your thoughts wander to

"*The Comforting Theory of Time.*"

*As she talks, your face
shows a polite concern,
but your mind starts to ponder…*

*How long could she
POSSIBLY keep this up??*

It's usually less than 30 minutes.

But what if??

But what if...she just had three cups of coffee, and is ready to keep me here for hours??

Could she talk forever?

That's when you remember...

It doesn't matter how it will end.

It doesn't matter when it will end.

The answer to your question is "no."

She cannot do this forever.

*As certain as
the passing of time…*

*This uncomfortable encounter
will end.*

*You are not stuck
here forever.*

Because time is a constant that she cannot control,

time will pass,

and one way or another, eventually this situation will end.

On that you can depend.

That's all you need to know.

And that's comforting.

(And besides…if she just had three cups of coffee, Mother Nature will be calling her inside shortly.)

(Wink)

But no need to pick on little old ladies…

(Grin)

There are plenty of times in our lives when we're uncomfortable,

and we just want "it" to be behind us.

Have you ever been...

stuck at an airport?

caught out in a cold rain?

locked out of your car?

or...
about to meet your date's parents?

*(This is when you really wish you **could** speed up Time.)*

Every one of these predicaments will end...

...because all things end.

Flight delays eventually pass.

Rain someday turns to sunshine.

Locksmiths arrive and open cars.

And sooner or later you realize…

...your date's parents weren't going to like you no matter which sweater you wore.

(You tried.)

Good, bad, or otherwise…

Life's uncomfortable situations gradually pass with the constant progression of Time.

*It's the comfort of knowing that it **will** end, that makes your situation so much more bearable.*

Not of knowing how.
Not of knowing when.

*Knowing that…it **will**.*

It's dependable.

It's predictable.

It's a certainty.

*The discomfort that you're in,
that you wish would end…*
will end.

That's comforting.

*But what if the
situation is a little "bigger?"*

What if you're...

facing surgery?
changing careers?
ending a relationship?

struggling just to get by every day?

These are difficult times.

These would all be difficult issues to deal with, and comforting thoughts might be hard to find.

Breathe.

Relax.

Calm.

Let the dependability of time free you.

This is when you remember that just like with the neighbor lady…

The comfort is not from knowing how it will end.

The comfort is not from knowing when it will end.

*There is a simple comfort,
just from knowing,*

*it **will** end.*

No one can stop that.

Time will keep moving forward.

*No one can make time
move faster or slower.*

*So, with the dependable
and constant progression
of time,*

*You **will** find yourself
on the other side of:*

*your surgery.
your career transition.
that bad relationship.*

    those darkened days.

Some how?

Some way?

Someday.

*It **will** happen.*

On that you can depend.

And that's comforting.

*The Comforting Theory of Time
has gotten me through
a lot of bad situations.*

Try it.

*The next time life hands you something uncomfortable to deal with, simply remind yourself ...it **will** end.*

Undeniably.

The "how's," the "when's," and especially those nagging "why's," are a little more manageable when there's an undeniable light at the end of the tunnel.

Take the breath.

Remind yourself.

It will end.

(All things end.)

*When the rest of life
doesn't provide one,
The Comforting Theory of Time
gives me something on which
I can depend.*

Whatever my uncomfortable situation, I know that time will eventually set me free.

I don't have to control it.

I don't have to do anything "to it."

*I don't have to
know how.*

*I don't have to
know when.*

*I just have to
embrace the knowledge
that it **will**.*

*(And remember
The Comforting Theory of Time.)*

*The certain and unchangeable
progression of Time
...will set me free.*

*The Comforting Theory of Time is **not** a call to **inaction**.*

It's not about ignoring difficulties or rushing toward resolution.

We must still

 ...rise to meet each day.
 ...keep moving forward.
 ...embrace the journey.
*...make the wisest choices we
    can along the way.*

*We do all of this while trusting
that Time is moving alongside us,
allowing it to do its work
as we do ours.*

*It **is** about*

...recognizing the quiet, steady inevitable rhythm of change.

...an invitation to trust that where you are now is not where you will always be.

It is a call…

to hope,
to calm,
to motion,

to movement, without urgency,
to progress, without pressure,

to letting go of trying to
"figure out the puzzle."

(For now.)

*There may be no perfect
solutions available right now?*

*What is available is the certainty
that time carries us forward,
(sometimes gently,
sometimes not),
but always...onward.*

This uncomfortable situation will end.

(All things end.)

*The Comforting Theory of Time
promises us that someday…*

*we will be looking back on this
uncomfortable situation,*

from a new place.

On that we can depend.

*So, in those moments
when your eyes glaze over,
and the voice
in your head says*

*"Am I going to be here
forever?"*

*Knowing with
undeniable certainty
that the answer is "No,
I will not be here forever,"*

that somehow, some way,

*time **will** set me free,*

is very,

VERY,

(You heart already knows what's coming)…

(Grin)

comforting.

(The End)

Dedication:

This book comes on what I hope to be the end of a very difficult time in my life. Only time will tell. (Grin) Whatever the result, I know the cause for my continued hope, and what seems to have been a triumph over my daily struggle, is, and always has been, my friends and my family.

Difficult times help you learn who truly loves you. My family and a few close friends rose to the surface as many simply ran away from the conflict. To those members of my family and those few who emerged as true support during this time, I dedicate this book to you with gratitude and the purest of loves. The love that you showed (and continue to show) probably saved my life. You were beacons back to my own true self. You led me back to the hope that I always held, even when I thought it was lost. To those family and friends - this is for you! To those many friends who simply didn't have the strength to be there when I needed them-perhaps you'll write your own damn book someday?? (Grin) But don't worry, if life turns the tables, I'll still be here ready to share my hope with you again if you ever need it.
(Wink) – **Gary Kilmer(2006)**

Afterword:

I originally wrote this book in 2006. I was awkwardly navigating my way through what I thought at the time was to be the most difficult period in my life. In that moment, I certainly couldn't imagine anything more painful coming my way, and my youth fueled naivete told me that only better days waited on the other side of my journey.

I wrote the book. I edited. I pondered. I edited more. The process of creating "The Comforting Theory of Time" was the project that got me out of bed in the morning. It was the task that gave me the strength to move forward, not always clear on which direction to go, just resolute in the knowledge that "forward" was the only option.

By the time I ended the project, a year had passed, my life had grown more manageable, and one day I simply "looked up" and realized that indeed, "time had set me free."
My uncomfortable situation had ended, just as my understanding of "The Comforting Theory of Time" had always promised me it would.

*I didn't want to go backward.
I wanted more than anything to just "get out there and live!" I wanted to celebrate and embody the joy that I had waited so long (and worked so hard) for.
So, I did.*

*As one of the ways I "moved on",
I put "The Comforting Theory of Time" in a box, and put that box in a closet.*

*It stayed in that box
for the next 18 years.
It is now 2025.*

In the last 18 years, I fell in love, created a home, had major surgery, almost died, learned to walk again, moved across the country, created another home, got married, got divorced, changed careers 4 times, fell in love again, followed my heart, had my heart broken yet again, and have questioned everything I've ever believed more times than I can count. Maturity now tells me; that's just this crazy ride we call life.

Through it all, "The Comforting Theory of Time" bounced around the back of my mind like a pot coming to a slow boil on a faraway burner. I began to realize that after working on it for so long, I had completely soaked it in.

*I didn't need it in my hands. It was in my head, and more importantly, it was in my heart. I'd spent the last 18 years embodying the concept. Growing stronger through every challenge, I had been reminding myself of the power of letting go, moving forward, and letting the dependable, unchanging constant of time carry me to a better day.
With nearly every challenge I had said to myself "This will end.
I will be looking back on this someday."*

*It was on a particularly difficult night only recently that I found myself searching for something, something to steady me.
And that's when I realized, I needed "The Comforting Theory of Time" in my hands again. I needed its calm, its rhythm. I needed the breath between the words. I needed the comfort that came from a slow and intentional reading.*

I fished it out of the box it had lived in for nearly two decades, held it in my hands, took a very intentional breath, wiped the tears from my eyes, and began to read.

That night I felt comforted.

The next morning, I decided to publish.

The message behind this story? Read this book, but don't put it in a box, don't put it in your closet. Keep it close.

Trusting Time isn't the same as waiting. It's not about standing still, it's about moving forward and staying in motion without panic, even in small ways. It's about making the best choices we can while allowing Time to work its steady magic.

Time moves forward, and so must we.

A day will come when you want to revisit "The Comforting Theory of Time." Maybe tomorrow, maybe next month, maybe in 18 years, but it will happen. It will be here for you when you need it, just as it was for me, because Time moves forward, and so do we.

And that in itself is comforting. As it always has been. As it always will be.

-Gary Kilmer (2025)

*****

As part of its initial launch in 2025, several hundred copies of "The Comforting Theory of Time" were gifted with a simple message and request:

"This book is my gift to you.
*If you find comfort in these pages, I encourage you to pass that gift along — **to pay it forward**. Send a copy to someone in your life who might need it: someone facing uncertainty, someone who could use a gentle reminder that time moves forward, and so do we. A simple moment of comfort, when shared, can travel farther than we ever imagine. Kindness creates ripples that, like time itself, carry us all forward."*

If you'd like to send this book as a gesture of kindness and support...

Please visit
www.TheComfortingTheoryOfTime.com
or scan the QR code below:

Notes:

Dedication (2025):

To Alison: *My "original in every way" muse. You taught me...not to take myself too seriously.*

To Suzanne: *My Italian sister. You taught me that "the right sauce"...can span more than 30 years (and counting.) Picture it. Sicily.*

To Paul: *You taught me...that true friendship and respect are worth holding on to.*

To Wayne: *You taught me...that kindness to others always matters. Always.*

To Keith: *You taught me...to write from the truth in your heart, whatever that may be.*

To Shawn: *Thank You. You taught me...that I had strength inside that I didn't know I had.*

To Matthew: *You are one of the ones that didn't run away. You taught me...to do my work, to face life's challenges, and to always be brave.*

To Mitchell: *You rose above and somehow always stayed "sooo Mitchell." You taught me ...to stay undeniably me. PS...Chicken French.*

To Geena: The bravest batshit crazy woman I've ever known. (Wink) You taught me ...what real courage looks like.

To "Doc" Chinnici: You saved my life and somehow gave my soul time to heal. You taught me...that pain eventually subsides.

To John & Larry: Though our paths have diverged, I remain forever grateful. You gave me safety when I needed it most. You taught me...to give and share generously.

To Carl and John: Always there for me when I needed you, you taught me...that sometimes you "just gotta decorate the cake!"

To Mark: Thank You. You taught me...what I need in life and how much I am truly capable of.

To Poly: Always quirky and true, You taught me...to support fearlessly. Hot Dog Pineapple?

To Megan: You are my person. You taught me ...to lead with Love and always make MAGK.

To Melissa: You are my lighthouse, always helping others. You taught me what it looks like to move through pain...with dignity and grace.

To Kimberly: *You are my hero. You taught me to live, love, and Be Optimal...all with Joy.*

To Michael: *Focused as a laser. You taught me...to keep my attention on what matters.*

To Seth: *WTF, Seth?? Turns out, those letters stand for "Wow. THAT's Fun?!"(Wink) You taught me...to smile from my heart. Blackbird.*

To Tania: *You called once just to say I love you. You taught me...to cherish the people vulnerable enough to be close.*

To Ernesto: *One text message from you sparked a creative fire in me. You taught me...simple gestures of kindness matter.*

To Mindy: *Quietly strong...you were my first example of someone staying true to themselves. You taught me...authenticity matters.*

To Dad: *You taught me...that being different is okay, and that loving one another is what truly matters. You are love. You are loved.*

To Mom: *You taught me...everything. Everything that I live, all that I am, and the north star that I follow, is all because ...you put it there.*

With Endless Gratitude, Gary (2025)

US Copyright
Registration# TXu 2-473-748
Filed: 2/14/2025
Literary Work: The Comforting Theory of Time

The Comforting Theory of Time
Trademark Serial Number: 99046525
Standard Character Trademark
Filed: 2/18/2025

The Comforting Theory of Time
Extended Distribution
Paperback Edition 5.5" x 8.5"
ISBN: 979-8-9927352-2-2

www.ingramcontent.com/pod-product-compliance
Lightning Source LLC
Chambersburg PA
CBHW032052090426
42744CB00005B/185